"Kenzie Allen's *Cloud Missives* renders as a child's face,' in poems that enact Ind profoundly embodied recovery operation ....ation and repair, twenty-first-century poems tha. .....id the work of the lyric into the territory of 'elegy against elegy,' love songs written to drive out violence and exoticization masked as love, and poems that wake to the desire to awaken. Along the way, there is exhumation in all its forms, of pop culture signifiers, from *Peter Pan*'s Tiger Lily to Indiana Jones, and revivified archetypes, from the ghost of the British Empire to the Evil Queen, harpy, fanged siren. Most crucial is the disinterment of personal scars and the violence they represent, and ancestral bones, 'piled, piled, / piled; *piled*; PILED; PILED, / nameless, done in, / piled—piled—piled,' each twisted foot and chipped skull a clue to an origin story and 'a keyhole / to let angels in' and the indefatigable voice out. Allen has written a masterwork of self-reclamation and survival through love."

—**Diane Seuss**,
author of *Modern Poetry*

"This incredible debut announces Kenzie Allen as an important voice in Native literature. Through impeccable craft, she explores themes of health and healing, Indigenous genealogy and identity, kinship and love. These poems are 'a song against the song of our demise.' May their missives travel far and wide; may their words bloom like sweetgrass."

—**Craig Santos Perez**,
author of *from unincorporated territory [åmot]*

"With archeological care, Allen begins a poetic and meticulous examination of the layers of life. Often surprising, these poems 'know violence / like it made me—rage, / like it rocked me to sleep.' Intensely scrutinized events that involve Native women are separated into strata to reveal a powerful self and a voice that seems to have been waiting beneath the pressure of years to, at long last, speak."

—**Heid E. Erdrich**,
author of *Little Big Bully*

CLOUD

MISSIVES

CLOUD
MISSIVES

POEMS

Kenzie Allen

TIN HOUSE / PORTLAND, OREGON

First US Edition 2024
Printed in the United States of America

Credit for poem epigraph on page 38:
"What Made the Red Man Red"
Words by Sammy Cahn | Music by Sammy Fain
© 1953 Walt Disney Music Company
All Rights Reserved. Used by Permission.

Manufacturing by Kingery Printing Company
Interior design by Beth Steidle

Library of Congress Cataloging-in-Publication Data

Names: Allen, Kenzie, author.
Title: Cloud missives : poems / Kenzie Allen.
Description: First US edition. | Portland, Oregon : Tin House, 2024.
Identifiers: LCCN 2024014798 | ISBN 9781959030607 (paperback) |
ISBN 9781959030669 (ebook)
Subjects: LCGFT: Poetry.
Classification: LCC PS3601.L4323 C56 2024 | DDC 811/.6—dc23/eng/20240402
LC record available at https://lccn.loc.gov/2024014798

Tin House
2617 NW Thurman Street, Portland, OR 97210
www.tinhouse.com

DISTRIBUTED BY W. W. NORTON & COMPANY

1 2 3 4 5 6 7 8 9 0

For those who make shapes
from every cloud

CONTENTS

LETTERS I DON'T SEND

LOVE SONGS

CLOUD

MISSIVES

LIGHT POLLUTION

Somewhere, cloud missives;
buckshot echoes devouring a hillside

in knock-kneed devotion. Elder rain,
a voice that tells each of us: *ache.*

Fill vast jars with the pulp of it, and
seal them with whatever tools you find.

We tried to obey, though muffled by order,
though every scenic outlook was already gone.

We tipped our throats to night showers
and tried to lick back stars the city had obliterated,

to resurrect anything at all by taste,
their glittering signs and warnings.

PATHOLOGY

The dead do not bury themselves

BREAKING GROUND

I enter the gravesite.
No catacomb, no bower,

the spade a blade shaking,
christened in the mound.

I have left the world behind
to find the world still

sheltered in dark.
I have brought my art

to witness.
The tomb, disturbed—

yet layer by layer, like papered
skin, pressed edges reveal

each basket of soil
with which they built the risen earth

to honor their dead, those who are gone now
caring for those who are gone.

What did I think to find
of my own history? Some reason

for my battered form? What of the memory
I carried, the almost-end of me,

arms to break, to lay me in the ground.
It comes easier outside myself,

the story I give
to the buried,

the salt on my tongue.

ASK ME HOW IT HAPPENED

There are ways to explain a lack
of warmth—rasp, tickle, absent
from the alienated limb.

The fish knife slices to bone
through tender nerves
on the left side of the finger.

Weight like horse hooves or granite
—in my case, composites of shale—
compress, shear, press into translucence

the skin, black and yellow and dead.
There is nothing between surface and interior,
there is nothing but pain, and then—

nothing, numb in concentric circles
from the wound. The body holds its secrets.
The body's maps extend a memory far beyond my own.

The arrow's fletching cuts the hand
once, and again, and again, and again—
and the habit forms

a newly silvered track.
No hurt can come from it,
so long as the aim remains true.

The molten glass that stayed
long enough to burrow deep
leaves stronger for its cicatrice.

My left knee with its moonfaced scar
can't feel you, dear. Yes, even now, even
when you press hard with a single pin.

PATHOLOGY

I used to have a depression
on the ring finger
of my right hand
where I would crush
a pencil against it
while writing. You tell me
the body makes room
for our favorite ways;
bones thicken like pearls
from the heft of a child.
The teeth will alter
their common alignment
to pocket a pipestem, to mention
malnutrition. The twisted foot
betrays a man bent in the mines—
the chipped skull is a keyhole
to let angels in. The cracked rib
healed over or partially knit
proclaims care or some survival.
The pelvic girdle a vessel, widens,
billows at its sutures,
whereas the male's remains
heart-shaped and rigid.
Were I left-handed, my right tibia
would be lighter and more slender.
Were I beaten enough, even this
would be written in my bones.

PIANO FACTORY

I

Another body worlds™ exhibit with bull's-eye
nipples. Another misfit superhero movie with artistic unibrow.
Some cologne bottle on a beach. A lipsticked diva
scowling in a hitler 'stache—
the work of sharpie warriors. Someone's tag
overlapping someone else's tag.
Advertisements were a way of making seasons
when I first arrived, series premieres and the overnight flop
and another sullen model, pasted up.

II

I'm at the bar where you last walked out on me, texting you that I'm
at the bar where you last walked out on me, where we fought
and made up, where I watched you drink too much, hoping it wasn't
another night for chasing each other down, past the piano factory
into the wet street, up and down 10th calling your name.

III

I ran then,
I guttered, juiced lozenges
to ribbons, I clacked the teeth hard
like a language; could beg more
as tender-bellied, soft-skulled
never-knew-better. Ducked,
still, I hid my claws in fingers,

my sharps in faulty cupboards,
I hunched, lurched, lingered.
Sometimes we ran the same direction.
              I can still see everything:
wrists knitted in fever,
tangled half-dark, our favorite alley
as breath in my bad ear,
the you of before leaving and
sometimes touching
more firmly than intended.
Hours irretrievable,
the incinerated bridge,
lit-up edges and city lights
a tempest, a murmuration,

pitch failing; failing;
lost. For how long?
The machine says *TILT*
and I do. I can't sleep,
can't sing, but the body adapts.

IV

They tell me men of your age never recover from loss, they burn
and pile and hate the passionate women as much as they adore them. I knew
the way a caress could crack a jaw.

V

        We congregate
around every grassy acre, we will find means
to feel moss. I miss the vinho verde, the kitchen
late nights at wooden tables where we all confessed

and took one another's portions, the balcony overlooking
small alleys topped with church bells and wire. But then,
I say, *I don't hate you.*

        The subway makes me sway like a willow
in warm breezes, the subway makes me aware of everything I touch.
A good dismount looks like never putting your hands on anything.

PSYCHOMANTEUM

For years, I'd believe
mirrors at night were portals, semipermeable,
housing shadow selves who only wanted
to make themselves whole through our capture.
That the light flicked on in a furious panic
would vanish them as though never there,
so bathrooms and even the windowpanes
could conquer me, could shiver my blood.
I carried no such fear lightless in bed
beside you for so much time. Months, I thought
I slept more soundly for your breath on me
as we shoaled and pivoted—all night, a school
of precisely two herring, wise to the currents,
each other's every restless turn. I learned
the rise in my throat, the acid-spark tongue
and tide rush of my quickened heart. I pulsed
new alarm and exit-seeking and pitch-black
comfort crouched behind couch arms or
slim as I could become around a doorframe,
mouth-open breathing so as not to be found.
It did not happen all at once. I did not claw
or seek weapons or speak so, so softly
at first, but became the wraith, yes, as I aged
into what time made of us, what the drink took
and molded, how night terror manifests
no longer in phantoms but in flesh and
muscle and don't you fucking dare, in ambush
and collateral, in every broken thing I'd have
liked to take with me, and there is no mirror
to reach through now—you've turned on me,
every switch, the room filled with brightness
I do not feel and cannot touch.

IN WHICH I RECALL THE FLOOD AS PINK LIGHTNING

To the boy who held me down,
said, *Shh! Shh! It's okay*, and later
took up with the Church—for heavenly glory,
not for what he did—I have no complaints.
I've looked for alone time, hours,
and only found brambles in the mouth
of an off road. I know your apartment letter
but not which floor you live on.
Once, I climbed on top of my sweetheart,
scooped in the seat of a white Ford
gritted and worn, and I said *Shhhhh*
and *shit* and *we have to get a backup plan.*

That night, the sand turned to cotton,
to sand in my teeth.

We get a plan. We get back in the car.

The grit turns to glass.

Every time I ask the elevators
to stop on my floor, I press the buttons
hard, like thumbprints in a browned thigh,
skin-memory ghosted white

like a lit-up MRI. Everything on my body
has been tested. Everything passed inspection
at one time or another. Now, my ring finger is twisted
leftward, and my wrists have toothy little marks
where something must have nipped
the derma deeper than intended, and
my eyes slip sideways when the room

brightens, and my nails never recovered
from bitten down to the quick, and these days,
I only wince when you're not looking,
and there's that one brown river swollen
over my open shoulder blades, which says
here it struck, here it struck badly, once,
maybe it will never strike again.

FORENSICS

The burial matters.
Fetal and twisted
fear their gods, and
there may be red ochre
among their possessions.
Arms over arms of the pious,
and the multitudes
heaped like netted fish,
and the whole house—
the kings, and the fan-bearers,
and the hunting dogs,
and the boats, and the rowers,
and his first wife, and his astronomer,
and his favorite horse in the ground—
splinters with the weight
of an eleventh snowfall.
You tell me there is meaning
hidden in their best clothes.

Everyone in those days fell to consumption,
and died indeterminate
of pathology.

When you examine me, years from now
postmortem, find the bone spur
jutting from my knee. Write "possible
limp"; do not be precise
with more than measurement.

Do not weep
for my childless ischium.
Put numbers in my name.
Do not imagine a face where there is none.

CENTRAL NERVOUS SYSTEM

Off the sidewalks, into the streets

What we have lived through settles
in the small axons, what we endure
whipped along vertebrae
all the way to curled toes.
We flinch, we fetal, we shrimp round the radiator,
we know the epicenter by the shock,
we know the limits by the scale of a grimace.
We know it doesn't end there.
We know our brains are dying from first breath,
and we know when we begin to die faster.
We gather, we breathe and can't
breathe. We cry *mercy*, we say *uncle*,
we say *don't*— like the wind
is sucked from our bellies too soon.
Or after years of the slow, dull pain,
we lip press, we whiten,
we shift our weight to the better leg,
press its heel to new damage
in our favoring. We buy every contraption,
back stretcher, compression bands,
the miracle sciatica cure and its clever pressure points.
We WebMD, we infomercial,
—we laugh it off!—we minimize,
except to say we must have deserved it.
We gather. We pray. We sing songs.
We ask anyone who may be listening
for a cure, for the way our pulse is tied to it,
our electrochemical innards, our brains, our eyes,
our fingertips, even that which we've long ago lost.
We plead. We gather. We pray.

We beg the doctors for any diagnosis.
We therapy. We learn to walk again.
We identify injury by the swelling.

DRAW THE HUMAN FORM

Each stretch births a compression;
ribs strain, and the diaphragm will descend
so lungs can expand.

Think of the torso like macaroni,
or a pillow you've punched in the side.
The frame an hourglass: its contents,

hinged. If the hip kilts toward the shoulder,
there's give somewhere;
human weight is so often akimbo.

Like busted tiki torches careen against a fence,
or salt cypress gives in rough wind,
the good dancers will chasm,

mirror their crumpled limbs,
a sickled foot on a good surface,
a life of training, boiled to mere description:

fire-dusted pinecones, revelatory,
brilliant in orbit—sometimes, named. A good review,
clipped out and pasted to coarse paper.

Lifting her into the air, the apprentice
can see string attached to her fingers,
crushed blue in the hollows of her neck.

DETERMINATION OF RACIAL AFFINITY

*Oftentimes, a skeleton exhibits characteristics of more than one racial group
and does not fit neatly into the three-race model.*

A shapely nasal spline, rounded maxilla
and that flick of a scalloped incisor—
in all likelihood, according to the chart on the wall—

we can't be certain, when only bone remains, but compare
ulnar length, mandibular jut,
these caveats of origin.

> I press my tongue to my teeth
> and find no curved hollow. I press my hands to my mouth
> and find no fuller jaw.

> The teeth on the table stay quiet. The zygomatic arch,
> gentle and inconclusive. All I know:
> her hands are smaller than mine.

Are the cheekbones prominent?
Is there facial prognathism?
What is the shape of the cranial vault?

Mongoloid, Caucasoid, Congoid,
alternate morphs for sun-soak,
overcast, sweet tilt of the sockets

> the way *Draw Girls around the World* explained ethnic realism.
> Make her lips large and full—give her beautiful hips and tiny shoulders—
> define her muscle *thus*.

They don't say it starts in the skeleton, in fragments of fragments
                    and the .002 gram that could be user error
              or could mean your ancestors carried you down the river

                                        in the cradleboard of everything.
Nothing mentions variability,
and how every time you look at that skull of hers, it changes.

How you can't pull off your own skin
and ask your body questions.

MORPHOLOGY

So, we're all revisionists.
It happened like this:

in the hotel hallway,
stripped of everything but scraps and begging,

and in your version,
you let me back in. I was not hurt.

I stumbled out for ice.
I was not suddenly so aware of my skull

as the start of negotiations,
or the due conclusion

any mouthy girl might warrant
saying *No*.

I open the abdomen,
pin the skin,

isolate the lungs,
the tender spleen.

I ready my forceps.
I begin to probe.

Perhaps he planted some wriggling seed
that might ruin me from inside out.

Will the hate in me become a siphon?
A sugarbush spout to let loose my inside,

the part of me still red
from waiting.

We never heal in our own time.
Maybe it's a kindness,

to have grown these jagged teeth
seeking throats, fingers,

groins which should have stayed put,
like pepper spray from the gums,

the gut twisting at every mustache who walks in this joint.
Maybe it's a care the upstairs has taken, to make me wary.

Maybe it's forgiveness,
to arm me with permanent venom, bile, a new morphology,

vision fading or still painfully
sharp, these lidless eyes,

to have already
held shadows close.

PHTHISIS

Even the Bohème girl could unearth herself
a candle, with her mender's hands and fading

torch song, a red-flecked kerchief clutched in
cold fingers as the most luminous way to die.

I am also a flicker, near-survivor of pillowcases,
swift rivers, reckless breakneck wheel-turns and

each city rusted out, each Hanover, Vienna,
Hell's Kitchen. My voice is all that is left of me. My breath

as carved by flight and sweat and fear. I am no Violetta,
except when I am—draped on my fainting couch,

alluring as can be managed in the stage lights that reveal
too much of my arms, too much of my reddened eyes.

The cavity is formed; my death is assured; I practice my final cadenza.
In shimmering flourish, I ask for my flowers' return

only once they are wilted, my nobility a triumph
in silence alone. Ask *me* who erased the sea.

I was an easy smile and unbruised. I was not so translucent
and then I was. A whimper waiting to happen.

A plague that began in the pile of clothes on a wet lawn in moonlight.
Once, I was even alive. No apology manifests my reappearance.

Like forgotten lyric, a pile of beadwork I couldn't go back for,
the barbs become a soothe. The flame, a dress form; the dire,

a lantern with unlimited fuel. Dark, eventually.
We live through more than expected,

then expire, I assume,
singing 'til our lungs give out.

REMNANTS

Sometimes they pierce the veil
and come over this way lingering

in the eyes of hungry cats. They speak
soft as wingbeats, they thunder

like loosed linchpins down rockslides or
they've had too much. You don't ask

what they're looking for, it's clear
from the skulls they've gathered.

You already know these ghosts,
as when you twisted into the smallest crevice

away from the trap-sensor cameras,
but something went off, a shot, a burst

of limbless light. And then you were
one of them too, craving the skin of the younger,

pressing your air into every mouth you could find.

HOW THE SKIN BRUISES IF YOU LIE THERE LONG ENOUGH

Can't submerge this dirigible below the floor itself,
cold wood cheek-pressed and so hard,
hard like anything else you might have wished for,
new reality manifesting blows as cold, hard,
sunlit expanse. It's like the time they said they'd find you
culpable for someone else's memory, metamorphosed
from wheat grain to sharp-beaked chicken,
from self-defense to all-out war
in the crescent moons bleeding from the forehead
and perfectly matched to your own little claws.
Said you'd do time, not him, and so you did,
two more years' worth of maybe, and the occasional sunrise.
And then sunsets like the atlas said they'd come,
finding empties, knowing now so well that word
empties, mapping a coastline fogged up, 'roid-ragey,
lot in my life as I had chosen it.
I check my nails for ridges, my toes for thickening,
all the signs of a good life gone scarce
with worry, or new business, those who keep me up at night
and in demand. Everything about me, brittle.
I thought rage at least sustained itself if not the body.
My finger still aches when it rains,
from bent back, from slammed on the edge of someone else's railing,
from *don't you ever do that again*,
from *you want this, you're asking me to do this, every time.*
Where are the rats for my minefield,
where do I end up in collapse?
What ditch calls my name?
Who will make me just a body, again,
what will I say the next time, to beg for the blows,
what will I bruise to be bruised,
how many years will I have to these small joys—

the way the muscles expand with repetition,
the rush of my lungs as I ask it,
the strength of my limbs.
And this domain; gilded, burnished, mine.

MANIFEST

REPATRIATION

If, pursuant to section 5, the cultural affiliation of Native American human remains and associated funerary objects with a particular Indian tribe or Native Hawaiian organization is established, then the Federal agency or museum, upon the request of a known lineal descendant of the Native American or of the tribe or organization and pursuant to subsections (b) and (e) of this section, shall expeditiously return such remains and associated funerary objects.

—NATIVE AMERICAN GRAVES PROTECTION
AND REPATRIATION ACT, 1990

Sun-bleached bone
and sticks wrapped with the skins
in which we loved them. Or nestled

and charred by the broken hearth,
clutching the wing of a swan
to ward spirits. Or

wormwood, beechwood,
cherry oak, pine
slatted and nailed
neatly under six feet or in hard times
even stacked above one another
so that the bodies collapse
like floors of ruined buildings, sighing
into the coffins below. Or

piled, piled,
piled; *piled*; PILED; PILED,
nameless, done in,

piled—piled—piled—
piled, buried over quickly in the night.

Or in personal collections,
in trophy cases, or in pieces, piled,
catalogued and inked with the smallest numbers
along the cranial spline,

packed amid boxes in the basement
of the Longhouse Museum,
until proper funding can be acquired
for a proper display. Red-taped and returned,
gathering dust, far
from the longhouses you knew.

HOW TO BE A REAL INDIAN

The first time someone asks you how Indian you are, lie.
On the blacktop, the soccer field, tell them
one hundred percent, your grandmother lived on the rez,
or you were born there, hooked up to machines running on bad
generators, in a bad hospital in a bad part of town. Say you dream in Oneida
at night, show-and-tell them rose rock and kachina,
give them exactly what they ask for,
the first time. Learn to read from that book
of the boy who falls in love with Minnehaha, invents
written language, discovers corn, and departs in a canoe.

In the third grade, when your class suggests "Ten Little Indians"
for the Thanksgiving theme, offer to teach them
the dances you don't know, but should. Swallow hard.
Imagine your ancestors, the ones you see each day
when you get home from school staring down at you from the walls
of your grandmother's house, draped in their turbans and regalia,
Tecumseh, Red Cloud; imagine their eyes—not sad, but fascinated
by the evenness of your buckskin fringe, the wild neon
in your store-bought feathers. Sing "Ten Little Indians."
Fan your hand across your mouth. Say, "how."

The second time someone asks
how Indian you are, embellish. If you find out your mother's mother's father
was the son of a chief, tell them your mother was a princess. Tell them
your mother sang you songs at night while rocking the cradle,
in her native tongue, but she's forgotten all of it now. Tell them your tribe
waits for you, wants to embrace you as one of their own.
Tell them you are loved by your tribe. Memorize
the names of the Six Nations. You always forget Tuscarora.

After all, there is an agency for everything.
Call the BIA. Aren't you on the list? Dawes, Allotment—
can't you find your grandpa? And at first, this is a wonderful game:
Metoxens and Doxtaters, Hills and the occasional Cornelius.
No Antones in sight. No compound-noun names.
When you find the man who might have cradled
your mother's mother's small head in his hands,
you must sniff out the whole line,
begat and begat and begat, married then divorced then
they split up the property and moved to Oklahoma.
All the people who passed down the blood,
the blood you wanted to be rid of, sometimes
the blood you wished could multiply.
Give them names. Tally up their fractions.

The third time you are asked how Indian you are, decide
it doesn't matter, exactly. Say, an eighth. Say, a thirty-second. Claim
to be Choctaw or Cherokee. Claim to be a princess, too. Talk about quantum
as though trying to find a way to name yourself.

Go back to the rez. Brenda's gotten clearance to open up a bar,
just in time for your coming of age. Take your white boyfriend
and play pool with him amid a cloud of smoke, where he will chat up
the locals, where he will talk about enterprise and fair trade. At the pow wow,
buy turquoise and the tail of a fox, and soft white cowskin
for your mother's moccasins. Eat frybread every day of your life if you can.
On the way home, a Chickasaw will sit down next to you on the plane
with his hair in two black braids and cowrie shells around his leathery neck.
Despite eagerness, opportunity, the sudden, improbable phenomenon
of two live Indians on the same plane together at the same time,
say nothing. If he says something first, stay quiet. Because you aren't just
two live Indians on the same plane together at the same time.
You're *one Indian and a fraud*, flying toward Delaware.

The fourth time, the fifth time, the eighth time they ask you how Indian
you are, your mouth is so, so heavy—let it hang open for a moment
so the spirits can enter. Let the woman who had your name and died
before you were born come into your body and speak the wisdom,
let her Grandmother Willow you. Let your head hang over the stump
of Chief Powhatan, ready to be bludgeoned by your own father
for love. Take Maria Tallchief into your limbs, eagle-graceful,
turtle-strong. Try to imagine your own face
on the face of a gold coin, the baby on your back
as recognizable as the way you point the way
and shut that open mouth. Make its flatness stretch
toward centuries of silence. Lead the men down the great river
to whatever they seek.

RED WOMAN

If I am blood-ruled, let it be
as every pinch of tobacco taken

from medicine pouches and forcibly tucked
under the white shirt

of a thirteen-year-old girl, now empty
even of prayer, or a girl

whose last sight is the river,
or a girl whose last sight

is the river, or a woman
whose last sight is

the anger even before the river,
or a boy, who grabs a knife

and calls the cops and tells them
his own description. I tell you, that's despair

I know well. I'm cuter with my mouth
shut. Sexy, with two black braids.

The words sound better
when I don't speak them at all, so they tell me.

I'm all anger and bad giver, a riot waiting to happen
in that short little skirt, they say.

They ask me to wash my hair in the river.
To see what it would have been like.

Smile, they say. *Those braids are dangerous.* They say,
Where are you walking so late at night.

IN WHICH I BECOME (TIGER LILY)

Why does he ask you, "How?"
Once the Injun didn't know
All the things that he know now

The way back from the fire
was so long. Three canoes'
worth of carving the trees

once I got that rope off.
I crackled, I snapped and
twisted and turned red

but was not also fire.
Once, I did not know
the good medicine,

what month the strawberry
peeks up from the path,
which animals were clans

and not spirits, which spirits
for which we left the meal
outside the longhouse door.

Once, I did not know my name,
though I knew the good cloth
they wrapped me in, the women

and their songs. No matter how tightly
I am chained to an anchor,
no matter which waterway I sail upon,

it is in the fields Mother calls to me,
always en route, FaceTimes
another pow wow,

another blood discussion.
I am brown in summer
like fish skin crisped in a pan

but never brown enough.
I love a man to Punnett squares.
I tear my own teeth out on unseen,

know violence
like it made me—rage,
like it rocked me to sleep.

These are not our lands
but the soil is good
for growing apples.

These are not our apples,
but the flesh is good
and crisp. Sometimes,

the rope was even a comfort,
like a bruise, visible.
Some nights, I wished for that

from him. But no one wishes
for the tongue-tie, lockjaw,
for the smoke signal to work only one way.

No one asks the red woman
what made her. Once I did not know,
and I asked, *How*

can one hurt a fire,
if the skin is already
bubbled and charred,

How can one wound
a wound, but it deepens,
with each new smile I learn.

ILLITERATE

In the dream,
culture is a locked door,
their fingers cracked
round a key ring
and they are your fingers,
torn knuckle
you remember splitting
across the apple knife
in your white youth.
In the dream,
they are bleeding you
to count the drops
that are dark enough,
your lips unfamiliar
with the words,
the most dire *she wants*,
try *i·akwa·wá,*˙ but it is
not yours, only dream and
unintelligible.
When she wakes
there are still no words,
the door is a tomb
and when she opens her mouth,
turtles emerge,
weak from birth, slow-moving
sad history, *onʌ olí·waku,*†
"in time all is dilute."

---

* "It's mine."

† "Just forget it when . . . , there's no telling . . . , forever"

DRESS LIKE POCAHONTAS, THEN LET'S MAKE LOVE

Tell him, you have not previously undressed
this notion. Your mother would say,
"how strange" or "the older guy?"
—or "remember to call it regalia,"
though all he wants is a costume.
You didn't object to Indian Girl for the Girl Scouts'
Halloween jamboree, a Hobby Lobby
approximation, hair in braids, befeathered.
Your mother did what she could
to help you fit in with the troop, despite
war whoops and tomahawk chop
and cardboard tepee backdrop.
Did you see the new carpet, black-veined
marble, and baked haddock in the casino
buffet? Did you hear Barbara in HR
finally wrote up Gene? Wolf Clan can't eat
wolf meat, and if we ever got hold of turtle,
you must apologize, leave that portion
and take extra of bear. There is still so much
to learn. Your dark hair as three parts of the soul
you must weave back together.
It will be many years before you bead
a new beginning, and many more before
your regalia is complete. But each time you return
to the cattails, the orchards, the longhouse, the rez,
you bring your ancestors home again. You say,
Namegiver, she loved me, she took my hand,
smudged sage like oil drops straight to the ceiling.
No buckskin would mention this, no faux suede captures
what cannot be claimed. *Just this once,* he says,
do a little rain dance. You are trying to say your own name,
but can't pronounce it; you are afraid your skin is turning
translucent. Wear bronzer. Wear bronze.
Go on and braid your hair.

Sometimes when I'm sad I think about Indiana Jones
doing actual archaeology. Setting up a grid system.
Settling tiny spears into the red clay
at every corner, strung white line
dangling above invited earth.

In this scene, he shakes hands with a cragged Cree,
whose face holds its own stratigraphy.
What is found there will be
time immemorial
disregarded—a land bridge
is far more appealing—
and in this one, Indy has a soft mouth
easy with apologies,
and the temple isn't always
coming down around our ears.

In this one, *Professor* Jones
(dashing in glasses) teaches
a whole entire class!
And without even once mentioning
the word "discovery."
The frontier, he reminds us,
is someone else's backyard.
He uses slides in which Native people
(who else) at least are
smiling. He uses the word *Diné*.
Says *she·kóli* to a woman with long dark hair
sitting in the chair's chair.
He does all the work he's asked to do.
He grades his own papers!
He applies for grants
and pins each rejection letter to his office door.

In this one, he is a young man
who does not pick up arrowheads.

In this one, he surveys the burial mound,
adjusts the transit with gentle hands,
maps each contour with wonder
before setting shovel to soil.
He Munsell-charts the colors of the earth
like paint swatches, the kind he put up on the wall
last week at his wife's (oh fine, my) request.

In this scene, he does not light the bar on fire.

In this scene, he ends the chase early
before the fruit cart is overturned.

In this scene, he looks out for his Indian guide.

There was that one time
he returned some glowing rocks,
generously, to their mother tribe,
so maybe in this one he stops at the entrance.
He does not force his way inside.
He carefully notes the condition of the site,
leaves the gold statues
in their glorious,
supposed disuse,

but what story would that make,
to leave a thing better off alone.

IN WHICH I BECOME (EARTH MOTHER)

Who did you believe you were
when you spread your hands? Said,
I come in good tidings, but even
your mouth tripped, sunk a shovel
into the skin of my belly,
carved and fractured and tore
land from my every land.
Call me sage woman, palette and canvas,
your planetary, primordial home.
Call me always quaking
into rooms that are not ready,
the good curtains set beside the sill,
and everyone's gone quiet,
everyone's looking for the source.
You say you admire the way I kiss
sky, how I forge each shining horizon
toward which you sailed or called
destiny. You long to conquer me,
when all I did was nurture you.
You ask me to provide, you ask
for my deepest core, my iron ore
and uranium, you demand to mine
my innards, my caves, my sanctum.
You beg me to bless you
with jewels, black gold, copper
veins—you force me to split wide open.
You insist I belong to none but you,
say my justice is too costly,
must wait until the end of this
next silver seam. Tell me what's valuable
in all my life, tell me what's better
if not this soil, the way the land forms
to the balled fist, all spiked ridges now

when pressed or curled in the palm.
Clutch it hard enough, it will even hold
that which marks you incarcerable,
the loops and whorls, the lifeline's crevice.
Hold it longer, let the dermis be the thing to break,
years and years and years, for she will defy you,
no matter how you try to keep her.

A DATE WITH THE GHOST OF THE BRITISH EMPIRE

He shows up half-drunk and handsy,
in a polo shirt with exactly six popped collars,
all seersucker and patterned in tiny muskets,
his shorts covered in birds who no longer exist.

It's five o'clock somewhere, and the sun hasn't set on him, yet.
He manspreads across three seats at the bar.
He orders mai tais, tries to tell you of a gin joint
in—where else—*Bombay*, where he left his best stereoscope
and twinned pictures of all the known wonders of the world
or all the known wonders known to him.

He's three sheets to the wind, brass telescope tuned
to the far-off, the dark heart, another beautiful territory
ripe for harvest, where brown-skinned men bend in the fields
and dream only of night; where women give up
the craft of their hands and bodies at his behest.
In his wallet picture-foldout, he keeps postage stamps
of every land he's ever held, even briefly, in vast array.

Things were peaceful, he says,
back when he was in charge.
A shame, they'd lost the Colonies,
so early on. She thinks of her ancestors who fought in that war,
who gave up their arrows for guns, who offered
white corn against white starvation.
What did the empire know of starvation?

That's why they call it a *commonwealth*, he explains.
For the common—wealth—see?
The next mai tai comes on a place mat made from banana leaf.

The bar itself, a cabinet of estranged curiosities—
yellowed teeth in jars, baby moccasins, carved African masks—
arranged neatly in rows and tacked to the wall overhead;

alcoves of mustached men hidden
behind velvet ropes and brocade curtains
delineated with poppy blossoms and tea leaves and
Chinese screens with tiny white faces;
around the room, every possible shade of ivory;

bronze lamps shaped like monkeys;
chairs upholstered in what might be monkeys;
mosaic vases holding ostrich feathers;
a model giraffe made of cow leather
with limpid, deep glass eyes. Every possible creature
taxidermied into open-mouthed surprise.

Such a fine specimen, he says of her.
He asks to put his calipers around her lovely skull.

His best of everything
belongs to someone else. *Malta, Minorca, Gibraltar,*
she rolls the names around in her dark mouth,
Zanzibar, Sarawak, British *Ceylon*
—*no,* Sri Lanka—Mumbai—Myanmar—
think of all the names lost to his sons.
Think of all the tongues
flattened and torn,
or tax, collected.

The beaver
skins. The elephant
tusk. The model armies
splayed across the map.

He doesn't ask her to call him a cab,
but, of course, she does. She bundles him inside
with his tartan scarf and tweed wool cap,
knowing he's so prone to cold. Even now,
heaven forfend she be blamed for his death.

He makes one last pass: A protectorate! A dominion!
Come, join the fold.

She whistles to the cabbie, shakes her head,
pats the door as it slides out of sight.

She turns back to the world and its own wonders.
The sun has set, and it is night.

TOKEN

So far, I've lost sleep, but not children.
So far, I've lost tongues, but not air.
Bought my voice in the institutions,
so far off-rez I *must* be
an apple. I've left this country
a turtle, have come back
red and barbed. Raised volume
in all the wrong rooms,
made a bad reputation
with all my sinew.
I stare at those coffee mugs
in the china hutch,
their Southern patterns, Ute
black and white lines
painted and fired
and not Oneida, but here—
and I, here, and not also
inside cupboards.
Beads all over the closet.
Practice my *yoyanláti*,‡ only true
if I, too, can manifest.
I leave the house an apple.
I come home a harpy.
The zoom no longer cropped
on my camera's lens,
but reframed, pulled back as bad acid,
the world's horizon sucked into vanishing,
and we see you, all high-rises
and the occasional generous park,
sweet-talk the ocean into terra-form.
Of course, the island's purchase

‡ "It's going along good"

would not contain destiny.
You build upon it, glass and curved steel,
nightlife, financial district, cab stations
for the hurried. Skywoman is not here,
the muskrats also buried.
Even the waves quicken, and someday boil.

IN WHICH I BECOME (SKYWOMAN)

Let me   grasp   roots   all around me
            to ease the fall.   Let the fall be

        gentled   by the teeming flock,
        their wings   tender, interlocked,

    let me mother earth   as the earth
    mothered me.   Let the children   forge

a new pantheon   between them,   a balance
of dark and light,   a history   given breath,

    formed from the soil at our feet.
    Let it not be made easy,   but be made

    beautiful,   waterways   treacherous and
            generous in their might.   I did not fall

    without purpose.   It was no mistake
which saw me   leave the sky;   this is the story

            in which I throw myself   into the blue
    with my whole heart, to see   to the world beyond.

        The world at my back names me, and so do I.
    Let me   make a new legacy,   a becoming to

tell stories about   around a strong fire,
She Who   brought the medicine,   nourishing our people,

inspired   the animals   in their goodness
to create   the land.   Let me be remembered

                              for all I made,   and
                                          cherished
                                              for all I gave.

ELEGY AGAINST ELEGY

What I've given up has walked my path
alongside me, marking time: footfall, drumbeat.

We say, *He's walked on*, far beyond death,
and we wish him good spirits, good journey.

When I walk on,
let me walk on.

· · ·

This is an elegy against elegy,

a song against the song of our demise.

Let go the need for ghosts as memory

behind glass, quicksilvered—

remembered, while standing before you—

we are not dead and gone.

This is an elegy against lamentation

that will succeed only by its nature,

where what's lost can be lost again

and never returned, not in the light of day,

not in the light you take with you.

Those who have left me

have left me so much.

                                             They are walking on.

                            .   .   .

I walk among all our relations—
the hooved ones, and the flying ones,
and the ones who swim

into cool, deep waters, and the ones who
blanket the grasses in their multitudes,
who carry their children's children
even in the womb of their mothers.

I walk among the garden
where our sisters' fruits nourish us.
They wrap their arms around any trellis

or stand straight and tall, or creep along
the ground with their gourds, their treasures,
which last months and months in the bitter cold.

                            .   .   .

                                          Marvel at this miracle:

petroglyphs survive
thousands of years of weather,
and point the way past
dangerous rapids,

painted water monster
as more than story.
A teaching:

                              extinction is not an Indigenous word.
                                        This story goes on.

                          .   .   .

Though he may crackle the ground
in his growing regard, I walk easy
under brother sun's light.

He crosses oceans,
kisses each edge of sky,
                    endless.

As grandmother moon
casts the world in silver,
she shapes every shoreline
                    as she goes along.
I welcome her into my body.

                          .   .   .

I leave out a plate for my ancestors.
I ask their advice in dreams.

Once, my grandmother came to me and said,
in a voice warm and alive:

                                        What will you give back?

                          .   .   .

You mourn her passing long before she's gone,
she who raised you up from her own
clay and loam. Her skirts cover your fields
in green pastures. She is still here to be loved,

her song as gentle, enduring
wind, carrying each seed
to new beginnings.

. . .

This is an elegy against elegy.

This is a celebration.

Somewhere in a field

the bones dropped lightly to earth

after every rainfall.

The sweetgrass bloomed for miles.

IN WHICH I BECOME (POCAHONTAS™)

What else would I paint with?
        I was the one singing, after all,
who tipped my throat
        to the Blue Corn moon, taken

with every flash of neon leaves.
        Each sycamore height
begets a swan dive. You,
        putting down your musket, for once.

A river changes course
        over decades, but here I am she is
still finding her delta.
        Dugout upturned,

I've lain down for it, whatever love left me
        captured—and
did I fling myself across that execution
        for bravery or despair?

But the seeds listen better when you speak
        their name, their creator.
You ask me only where to find the gleam
        for which you came—

all this way!—with dwindling provision.
        What you seek won't feed you.
Is it only our animal companions,
        and their animal companions,

left, here, to humanize us? It did no good
        to say you can't own it, with this face.
Some never believe a smoke rabbit
        until it comes to pass.

Maybe that lung's catch isn't expansion
        but tension, a sudden snap as the system shudders
a prismatic release of the breath
        you didn't know you were holding for days

—which, like me, like all I know,
        is also a metaphor.
You look at me like before contact,
        like mist still lay between us.

I was buried that very first day.
        Why do I dig myself up again and again?
Maybe some things have gone
        too far now—

pastel winds, those bomb-ass leaves and sketched echoes,
        ghosts I'd never thought to become—
if not powerless, why *this* name still on the lips,
        why do I still look for faces in every tree?

You ask for a glimmer of fortune.
                        Like pillared light
whispering good advice,
                Corn Sister rises,

tall as flagpole or mizzenmast,
                        her generosity
the exact color of your thirst.
                We call it maize, I say—

I open the husk

like a prayer book.
I have no other coin to give.

I rise to my feet, kiss her leaves.

No metal, no discovery;   sustenance,
nothing of your desire.

But isn't it also gold?

Doesn't it also shine?

LETTERS I DON'T SEND

1

Let me remind you of who I once was
when we met: my arms with their savage blood

in its right place, the path of my fingers
unaltered. In the photographs, I smile

all the way to my eyebrows.
Hadn't rusted out my own voice box,

hadn't lived on enough floors to really know comfort,
knew nothing, clean as a suburb

with its spiked fences, automatic gate.

She had decided at last to become the villain.
Floor-grasping sequined lamé

on offer in Joann's bargain bin,
smoke bombs handy in the basement

where he'd left his stash of pyrotechnics
and an empty plastic whiskey jug—

even the crows seemed cooperative,
now drawn to the shine of her malice.

Her fingernails sharp.
Narcissistic and manipulative,

weren't those your exact words?
She becomes her own reflection.

She asks her reflection
what's fair.

3

Of course, there was rebellion
in the household. Discord in the sleep cycles,
one too many DUIs;

dig the hole deep enough,
even middle-class money can't get you out.
The time I gathered my birthday cash

from its every hidey-hole,
days after my clothing spangled the lawn,
bright and sodden,

having flown in the night
from the second-story window
as you took your evening smoke—

after the time I called you a hack—
and I drove all the way downtown,
twice, to bail you out. The evil queen

raises her velvet hood over starry diadem,
her teeth are arrowhead points,
looking ever more the shrew

every morning she sleeps in.
Her voice is the snap of lightning
in heavy rain, her body is pliant.

Her dark powers decrease
the longer you speak to her.
Sometimes she waits up late

asking when you'll be home.

4

Somewhere upstairs, Marilyn and Joe sit down
to discuss their grievances.
Her beautiful legs crossed toward the door;
he doesn't ask to smoke, just lights one up
and goes down the list. *That damn skirt of yours,*
always saying hello. Barely saw you,
but everyone else gets an eyeful.
They wallop each other with foam swords.
Marilyn flings herself backward, eyes closed,
and Joe catches her. *In my past life*
I was Cleopatra. Joe's past life involves a sandlot;
sometimes Joe dreams only in shades of grass.
Joe wallops a little harder this time with the foam sword.
Tell me what you were thinking. Cut the hyperboles.
Marilyn tries to explain to the tune of "Happy Birthday."
Joe defriends her (on the facebook). Joe says,
I won't wish you a Happy Birthday, because
you never wished me a happy anything.

5

And to the crows I must apologize.
No one told you of your rottenness
in a language so familiar, *succubus,*

> *you are the devil's attendant—*
> so that you grow to hear it in the stone corners
> and every man's voice thereafter

> and you understand your nature as prescribed.
> You are not the raven they make you,
> *quite sociable and forming strong bonds,*

you are more than a dart or a pin in night's blanket.
But let her exile have companionship in the remaining stars,
the saguaro and its breathing skin,

> the field itself—
> what better friends for the wicked
> than the shrewd, the nimble, the flock,

> black patent where their feathers press tight
> against her mantle, against her soft throat,
> black gleam of dear black eyes.

Some mornings, the queen emerges from her bedroom
bleary, bruised, sclera   spangled in red
where capillaries burst from sudden force—
all the outward signs,   sparing—

skin paler than she's ever seen it,
a bone china
patterned in blue and gray.

She enters the golden carriage, surveys her domain.

Did she know there'd be grief
lingering in those lands?
Crying all over the countryside,
wheat fields bent low, forests gone fallow,
thatched-roof houses drooped in rain,
relentless   rain,

a storm, she's told, surely of her own making.

And yet, I remember
those many days of downpour
as welcome friend, my own likeness
shown back to me, a sky I could finally recognize,
be recognized by,

a garden of cinders.

She wanders the deepest woods she can find.

She makes her offerings to the earth.

7

How you were doing things
for you now, how for once
in your life it was time to be

selfish, as though you had
never done such a thing
before. How you couldn't

think of anyone but the one
who would carry you as
you would carry you, as if

saving this sapling would
spontaneously engender
a forest. And the forest

grew thick in ugly days,
evolved thorns, all the wrong
enchantments. A forest of you,

every twisted form
a bad memory, and I
became the thistles,

the needled carpet,
the scrap of red plucked
by such hands—such

greedy, sidelong branches—
the castoff, forest leavings,
the lungs and the liver, taken.

8

Sometimes I think about all the times he almost killed me.
The whip-skitter knee-hug ride through Vermont at night,
So help me! So help me! and tweeting my last tweets
like some millennial asshole, but who could I call
after I'd exhausted every family member or friend
who carried my things out the door only to know
I'd carry them in two weeks later.
Kicked down the stairs and then hands at my throat
and the shaking. Fast air like a whistle and the pop and the shhh
as tympanum finally gave way. The blows to the soft round space
between skull and spine, the dizziness almost sweet
for it was real, more so than the words
you cannot love;
      you are heartless;
        you ruined my life;
          you ruined your own.
            You did it to me, too,
which was also some real. There were no clear rumors
in all that fog, but my eyes went blank,
nights I pinched and shook myself, said stay awake
for what may come. I gave as good as I got
when I could. I tore hair, I scrabbled and twisted,
I even slammed to the mat a few times
when my grip was solid and my ear still aching.
Sometimes I stared at the knife rack.
Sometimes I still do.
The evil queen is indeed heartless.
The life from you she squeezes,
and her hands are steadier than mine.

9

Two years from fortress covered in thorns
and one last drive to the airport,
she asks the mirror, again.

The beard she finds does not move her.
She has no wistful left for the line of the jaw.
The only empties are the ones she keeps

clustered for recycling.
The fog abates, dreams
less troubled by the day.

The queen has glimmered obsidian to moonstone.
Her wicked crown, once sheared at each point,
now, tendrils; the cold rubies, now diamonds,

however flawed. I don't even falter
as I flick past your pictures—
not anymore.

It's as though she never loved him at all
when she finally sent him to the forest,
as though she did not listen for his footfalls

or the sharp note of his axe,
but from the beginning coined spells
to ward every entrance, shaped a cattle grate of briar.

But no, there was an augur, here.
There was a poisoned well. I still tremble
at tenderness. I still look for any door I can find.

10

We talk about bad apples
like we each know one intimately.

If an apple awry
twists from the branch

into unrecognizable tartness,
dappled like horseflesh

pitted and gnarled, hard and crabbed
or a color he never expected,

it can't be the tree that made it so.
The mother only births herself over again.

Devils sprung from her limbs
dripping bad blood, bad little fruits,

inevitable, sure, but less a problem of genetics,
more a nuisance

of boll weevils, bruises,
what you'd half expect,

the outside getting in,
and one bad baby spoils the bin.

Even when it's daylight,
we light fires.

But here I am, glittering daggers,
my robes a night without moon.

The earth will move to swallow
what has long ruined me—

because we never lose our power, even banished,
even as graves turn slowly into castles—

I am the well and the gate.

11

Time heals, so they tell me.
Then I'm Yoko, green fairy, lit-up coiled harpy

siren-clinging to the bare rock—
all fangs. I shrug off skins like a cloak

when it suits me, and my dark powers flourish
with each selfie; I have become

the *yamauba*, mountain demon woman,
and all I feel is nothing.

I'm Meryl *and* Goldie,
my spine can twist like a ribbon curl,

my belly an opening you could reach right through,
but I endure. Survival is what really scares you.

The lair can lie vacant,
the rocky cliff sunlit and the waters

green into calm, for at last, she is Circe untethered,
her ankles a wildfire, her reach eternal and vast.

We will devour every legend
you tried to make of us.

I am already
a new constellation,

all my daughters
tending the stars at my feet.

LOVE SONGS

PALM READER, FIFTH AVENUE

As if everything in the world were penetrable,
we seek out archways, sweet lockjaw
of crook and clavicle. Even the ear is a marvel

of vulnerable invention. As if sanctuary,
your hand on the trapdoor of my skull
where *hush, quiet*, black boots clip the lintel.

What leaves these lines? Haunted rivers
parched in the palm. Line of Saturn,
Girdle of Venus, that break toward the thumb

a sickness. Someone might have hurt you once
or again. I want other hands, give me freckles on a white body,
you can dye anything uncomplicated.

Constellate me, flatten out the creases,
a nebula whose only clear picture, infrared and cave-like,
billows, birthing stars. Give me no other side

to these steel clouds, this cathedral.

LOVE SONG TO THE MAN ANNOUNCING
POW WOWS AND RODEOS

How your voice over salted flanks
licks tender, and when you say *young ones*,
our future, hitches left like making room,
and when you name the horses, booms low,
storms a kick-up moan, chases them down,
as spotted silverfish in a round pen quarrel
then shoot back out the entrance,
spotlit and away in a shuddering.
Name me a jingle dress in neon and gold leaf,
bespeak moccasins for my turning feet—
with my mother's best beading—
paint her having sewn those seeds
onto leather backing all of my life,
welcome the crowd to my birth
and the language to my ears, early,
my name, early, *wampum* and
the good spirits everywhere and early.
Don't send me home without a round of applause
if not a title, if not a good ride and a fast time.

ALL I NEED TO KNOW ABOUT LOVE I LEARNED
FROM MY FELLOW PRIMATES

Those who study marmosets will tell you:
wait, just a moment, beyond the rustle of leaves

as one goes by, you can hold your breath—
its mate is sure to come after.

I never imagined a pairing for life,
a call like a favorite song,

yet here we are, preening our chosen
on each limb curving from the bough

behind the glass. Or on the park bench,
or nestled in the highest place one can reach.

Titi monkeys, too, pair-bond in principle; in respite,
they stay close and note the absence of the other,

tails twined together below their branch
as if the body were a hand with one finger

longing to interlock. Alas, for the *man of the forest,*
Pongo pygmaeus, he travels so often alone.

Maybe it's just his way, or the city's encroachment,
as power lines cut through the trees.

The ringtails with their soot-black masks
pile up arboreal and warm

in what scientists refer to as *lemur balls,*
queens surrounded by their harem.

There will be dances for dominance,
a pecking order toppled and revised again,

in the flurry of lion-tailed macaques
leaping from tallest rock to lowest ground and back,

kings deposed in sudden upsets
common to their species.

There is the way the children are carried dearly
by father, mother, perhaps the whole troop.

How we and the orange-furred orangs
tend little ones the longest.

How our teeth are not so different, adaptive and broadly used—
same sensitive mouth, same flipped lips to bare anger or grin.

The gorilla who cradled an orphaned kitten all night in his arms.
The bonobo who saw her mirror-self and shied away.

The teenaged chimps throwing kiss-and-tell parties in the canopy
in wild exploration. I've learned to close my eyes

halfway to pleasure as furrows are scratched into my back.
We all have our little joys, our quickenings to rage,

our lairs and what we make room for within.
We cleverly co-opt whatever tools might come to hand.

We mourn, and cower, and beat our chests.
We press our face to the window and try to make out exits

or the faces peering back. We search every territory, every meadow's edge,
for those who might welcome a bite to the neck.

Maybe we delude ourselves, that we'll only need the one
in a life fraught, a world imperiled,

a habitat slowly, and quickly,
reduced to ash.

Somewhere in the dark,
a man grips his pillow girlfriend hard.

A man settles his hand on my thigh
like a lithe tail extended,

but I turn away for better sleep,
only to dream of the closeness

of leaves, of the emerald light
flickering over hours, fading

into a forest, shared.

LOVE SONG TO THE ALPACAS OF SOLOMON LANE

You know nothing of stars.
A low black river borders the field,
and a sturdy little fence you arch across
with your precious skull and your ludicrous eyelashes
should a child approach with carrots or careless hands.
You don't know the ocean, or the end of that road;
the bubbling cloud of ash thrown up by dirty bombs;
what a human can do to another human
or to anything else, really, that gets in its way;
the piles of glittering shards left over
from the jeweler's perfect cut.
You don't know the way they call us
gone, don't know life as *illegal*.
You've no concept of the delicacy of a vein,
which countries' lost water sends alfalfa to your bin.
If there is a hum overhead, some cold flying spider
crowned in a tiny green light and a single, relentless eye—
you need nothing of coordinates, demographics,
the outline of a district or illusion of safety,
just shears at the right time, a firm hand, a soft voice,
carrots, someone on the other end of a shovel.
The dense shag of your shoulders won't hold
the heat of this city. How many years until you are gone;
your pen a water feature in another speculative neighborhood
with houses all bricked in the French style
starting at only one-point-five million and
I look for you driving lonely the nights I come back to Texas
as though *from here* is belonging.
Your jaws work idle, your little hooves muffle in dust.
Would that I could have lived happy in your oblivion,
not seen airplanes and mistaken them for comets,
not seen so much I learned to want or fear—

but teach me, sweet soft-lipped faces, sweet big dark eyes,
how to settle my restless legs beneath me,
to be quieted for what I can have.
Low on the horizon, that flickering light—
I know it's not a supernova. A satellite will do.

ODE TO LOOKOUTS AND LIGHTHOUSE KEEPERS

And you imagine him with no family, but
he had a family with him, once, lovers

of adventure, quiet, the wildness of that realm.
Picture the mountain with all its greenery intact.

Picture the fjord as a mirror filled with sunset.
Someone had to shepherd each league and fathom,

to guide lost ships and guard the trees. Let me be loved
for my eyes, for my careful hands and all they can carry,

a marvelous dexterity over small instruments
—sextant, fire finder—an understanding of when

to sound the alarm—the radio, the foghorn—
or when to watch, wait, notate, ascertain

azimuths and distance and peril. Most days,
nothing happens. You wake at dawn,

and the tower is patient. You take up your tasks.
A simple life is all you've been seeking,

and here it is—make coffee, clean the windows,
scan the horizon, now and again.

You wait. To report, take weather, to brush your teeth
again, for mornings and evenings and visitors and no one.

For the bugs to leave, for the bugs to return.
For the cooler breezes, for the deep cool of night

and the lights out there in the dark sea or forest
that tell you there's something to work for,

someone to look for, a people to serve.
You wait for disaster to ease the waiting,

sparks, storms, spot fires and capsized boats.
Some you can help, and some you can't reach,

a coastline or cascade ridge you map by heart,
though it takes many days, many seasons' return.

You abide the boundless repose. You cultivate a gratitude
each day of that calling. You keep the lamp burning

for whatever might be out there still, reckoning the darkness.
There may be a manual hidden in the desk drawer, but

you learn by doing. Given meager supplies,
dropped by dinghy or donkey in the middle of mostly nowhere,

you make your way as best you can.
No more is expected but this and

a bit of think-on-your-feet. When the occupiers came,
the lighthouse keeper became

a watchman of another kind. The reserve boys
prayed at night and painted the walls with pinups.

The lookout called in air raids, as though water drops
and smokejumpers were not also an air raid.

You say, who's to say whose place this is.
You'd give it all back if you could.

I know you do only what you're asked
with a care for the lives in that glade or ocean,

a home you've made in making peace
with all the land and sea and sky.

WITH THIRTEEN MOONS ON YOUR BACK

for the desert tortoise

like tree bark curled into whirlpools of stone,
burrowed under earth while the sun burned down

and Coyote roamed the sand—do we, too, return,
each to our dens in the shivering dark,

wear armor as a shelter we can carry,
don't we, on your back, touch earth?

Sometimes, ever so slowly, we learn of the sweetness
of cactus fruit, mesquite grass, the arid wind

as the sound of an ocean rustling in creosote,
what the long-awaited rain can yet resurrect.

Coyote watches. He marvels; what small wisdom,
your survival, in this rising heat,

in this strange home you have made.

LOVE SONG FOR THE END OF US

In the great die-off, the fireflies will become fewer still.
The jar, empty. The hills and exultation

dark. Vestibules crawl through the shape of an arch,
slowed, then dead, memory locked to the last survivor

and whatever stories they told; a cardinal returned each summer,
vanished. Perhaps my children brown in the ultraviolet.

Save any space you can.
The hum of June buffets the doors not so long before we mourn.

There was a garden. Something to pray for, even at the wake.
I want to say it was enough.

I shudder to think of the bear trap shattering bone,
his tender paw gripped in a mouth he should never encounter,

or the gills cut through clear with filament
sharp as invisible; lipless fauna surrounded by fire

on every shoreline. We've seen so many
feathered stomachs filled up with ash;

beyond doubt, no air is left—
yet the breath leaves.

Only the lights on the sidewalk tell you
anything is left to be open to be left.

The flame hailing from the sill
in candle, holy water, paper stars—

that's the tongue of this house laid bare,
wide and beckons welcome.

I have prepared the linens.
I kissed a prayer to each crevice

like cupped hands, a flower pressed
brief and capsized by midafternoon

bad deeds done by strange fingers,
as though you don't know where you've been.

WHATEVER IS THE MATTER

My thought at the collarbone:
how the skin carries its light.
One breathable membrane,
an onion nerve-filled and luminous.

One half current-ridden circuit,
one hollow for these shoulders, curled spine.
Wrists undamaged and strong ankles,
free of any hurt. How I regret not opening

my mouth, the down-lit cast of my glance
where I studied that quality, sun-runner,
gold-bodied, how could I answer you
with all this earth piled on my tongue,

your limbs just stripped of anger,
how could I say, yes, there is something on my mind
rushing up as river in a locked car—voice-ruined,
could I explain the meteor in my chest cavity,

could I cluster verbs into sardine cans
and twist the lid back on and tamp it shut
with the silver pestle of my must not say
that which huddled, parched,

as we said, goodnight,
see you in the morning,
don't stay up too late.

LOVE SONG TO BANISH ANOTHER LOVE SONG

One nail drives out another.
My hammer was ready
long before my hands.
How a waning moon
betides a crescent,
how I knew, after
the deluge, the quake,
the sickbed, the all-body bruise,
I needed *kindness.*

The edge of the lagoon forges
the lagoon; the withered leaves
beg water—but not
a drowning, upended sky,
river weeds as only refuge,
entombment in the silt.
I awoke one morning
with a need to awaken,
as though I could smell flowers
distant on the wind, the end
of endless night, the fog
no longer filling up the brick.

Where was the mortar?

I craved the open field, a fallow
berth in which to birth
myself. What I thought fit me
only fit the outline of fear.
If I was *unlovable*, I became
unlovable. If *unworthy*,
I became that, too.

But in a sunset hours from my own,
I gave myself back to the flock,
dipped my tongue in a new mouth
ocean-deep. Some days,
I say you saved me.
But it was my tread at the doorway
and out into the road.

Whose kindness did I need?

A sandbar lines the cove.
The beaten path defines
the cultivated clover patch.
Above me, a swallow kites its wings
to the angle of the incoming
gale. My lodestone, once,
broken, the ink of my map
a ruined blur, undone
by the flood I'd thought to outrun,
a rabbit with no thicket,
only the concrete hollow
of an open storm drain. Only then
could I hear the nearby stream.
Outside, the lavender, the bees
greet each thistle, gently, the sun,
a break in the trees. Birdsong,
a clarion, kulning, invitation.
An apple, fallen right at my feet.

RIBBONS

How the doorways became ruined mouths
once a mistake had been made. Their gables,
arched lids or drooping stares.

        The streets of Lisbon, lonely.

I looked for you, but it was not a working number.
It was dark wine over a thousand-dollar rug
in shaking hands. *Grip that table*, I said,

        hold her like the earth moves.

Those other days: an alone dream
into which I let the city whisper a void.

        Of what in me was not empty.
        Of where the taxis will not go.

I was not ready to want you,
but now I am.

        On the day you came, I lived a pale blue
        dream in which I spoke perfect French.

        Now my tongue is my own again,
        past and present the same, sweet thing.

My mouth turns to film, cloudy, flecked—
it captures whatever it can:

        a cathedral, dust motes lit up in every color;

        a shop window holding a dress made of wire;

alleys with cobblestones softened by rain;

a cascade of pink bougainvillea;
me, smiling bright and full and free.

My ashen fingers quick on the tessellations, a river,
which resembled an ocean but was not an ocean.
I let the hillside lead me.

Rooftops and tile, everywhere.

Your skin, gold as good clothing
pinned to a line within reach.

CONVERGENT EVOLUTION

In a city of seven hills,
you told me once, *there is no fate*—

kismet: *a coincidence*
we mistake for grand design.

Could they be one and the same,
I asked, knowing

I was reaching for something
I didn't understand.

Say we're the same species,
but I never know what to believe,

faced with distance; alienation
more familiar to my skeptic's mind.

We're able to mate; and do.
But what can I make of your body

so unknowable to me, this anatomy
I can't capture, no matter how

my hands seek out the edges of you
to make reminders I could map—

a changing form, a grand design—
to learn your next bright incarnation.

Must there be rain in this poem
to approximate my longing?

Then let there be rain. A greater flood.
Let us grow into creatures that survive it.

There's a word for nature's need
to evolve a crab: *carcinization*;

as though his shape is best desired,
a sterling vision in this habitat,

the clay supple and sumptuous and easy
in the hands that make us whole,

and there are many crab-like shapes called crabs,
who aren't, in fact, true crabs at all.

We run out of names for the remnants.
We call them by their carapace.

I scuttle toward your chitin'd frame, similarly clawed,
yet drag along my chosen shell;

protection, refuge, home.
What can I make of us

without leaving my shelter behind?
Unless you were the nacre'd cove

all along, a foolproof cavern
fitted to my shoulder blades

with room enough to bend—
to huddle, coil, retreat—to shift

as the silver ring we sized and re-sized
for weeks, once you asked for my name,

until it slipped past the knuckle but twisted
round the phalange, loose enough to turn inward—

and we call that as good a match as any.
I wear that band, still.

Maybe you are not the catalyst
edged as my own edges, warded key in lock,

no meniscus of exactitude where water meets air,
but a grotto I grow into, a grove I learn

to inhabit. If you are the burrow, not the burial,
let this be the last shell I'd ever need.

In sand, and sea, and willowed grasses,
I would find my way to you.

ODE TO PUDDLE JUMPERS AND CHICKEN BUSES

Amid the rattles and jolts, in my dream,
my mother is stuffing her mouth with silk.
How much can you fit in a thimble, she asks,

                                                  degusting the loveliest scarf,
                monogrammed with my name—an heirloom, so she says.
                             What heirlooms have I to offer?

              The seats unmoor, the bolts unglue, at any moment
the whole chassis   might well be thrown
                                                down a cliff.
          Round the bends, sometimes you pray for your life,

                                   sometimes you marvel
                    at the mountainous green or white
                        beyond the windows.

     A kind of home
     I can hear coming, creaking fit to split me
                                 wide as no room allows.

               In the back, a burst of clucks and caws:
          a small party of farmers hailing from rows 10–12.
                Clacked knitting needles, too,

                a trio of scarf ladies, all elbows
nearly interlocked,
                                    furiously weaving

crabbed hands   and small,
homely motions
             forming a new scarf from rough ball of yarn.
                I fall back asleep, but no yarn is eaten.

Lord, the smell,
the crowing

of where to find the best

ice fishing, mangoes,

roadside stands full of kitsch.

I look for my mother. I want to tell her
to look out the window.

A turbulence beckons,

a crazed horizon,
everything's gone so far sideways
it might roll right over,

the air so full of updraft
I've heard it described
as a minefield of elevators.

Soon as I'm arrived

I want back up again—

I can almost understand my place in it

where all I can see becomes

circles and lines,
silos, irrigation, the winding crevice
thickened up in snowmelt,

the smallest tributary
threading through a valley
long before I arrive.

Surprised any green is left.
Everything is a floodplain eventually.
But the spaces are there now.

To the rez and back again,

                                                   the small places

serviced by the smaller planes,

let there be paths   among the thermals,
the sudden tractor beam,
let the driver have mastered it—

jarred comfort, teetered calm,
                        the wild roll of the chicken bus,
lulled in crashed up against
and I suppose I did that   all my life.

WHEN I SAY I LOVE YOU, THIS IS WHAT I MEAN

Perhaps these words, too, will vanish.
The electricity will fail, memory cards
corrupt; the generators run down
and even the pages decompose
eventually, or burn. I am no Greek
kept alive in libraries or the minds
of curious men, these equations I write
not vital to our survival or progress.
My telomeres will weaken. I'm not immune
to age. And if I want it remembered,
the way you asked my skin to sing for you
or how your scalp locks the scent
of Oregon, the lookout tower, the flames
just past the horizon, I can't hold it
or make it stay, no matter how clever
my pen, my fingers at keys.
Your arms will fade from knowing,
the particular blue hunger of you debauched
in the confine of colored ink.
Somewhere, there's a museum of best mixes:
azure, lapis, mummy, and ochre,
lined on shelves in glass vestibules,
preserved for future study.
There are interns dusting each collection,
responsible for keeping the markers
in good repair. So, if I am the servant
whittling time, only to have it return
out of knowing, if my body stains the air
and settles on cruets or seeps into rags
to become the perfect brown
dunes and their shadows, my innards
the crimson cloak on a worshipper,

if I am the pigment and the vessel,
why not blue? Why not the light
through the fogged air of that mountain,
why not memory engraved in something
stronger, a stone arrow to arms
that were, and are, and are good.

QUIET AS THUNDERBOLTS

And I kept it from you like a kill,
my name, my legacy, my shoulder chip
and the small hollow beneath

where I can be wounded. The Longhouse
I whittled to matchsticks, abalone
filling up with hair ties, coin-bank

buffaloes and iron turtles a pan-flash
of identity, an almond eye watching
from between the white bookcases

and photographs of cities, orchards,
graves. A lonely ironing board
left to the street outside our old place,

candles I lit in Lisbon for all the women
I have loved. Animals who are no longer
with us. Animals who are no longer ours.

So much landscape I can't tend to,
wide as a child's face
and crumbled in drought,

rimmed in salt. I kept the Water
Lily, how Bear Clan was given
the medicines, Namegiver,

how she made me darker
with her words. The turquoise ring
and how it pleases the Spirits

to give that which has been
so admired. The sweetgrass
in my sock drawer, the exact volume

of air I can fit in my lungs and belly
as I try to swallow and breathe
its sweetness. Every bead, every

loop of every treasure necklace—
I kept porcupine quills
in my throat, I let the water drown me

every night in my river-bottom canoe.
I've been sleepwalking
since I got to this earth,

since they brought up the soil
and made an island, those who did not perish
in the dive. Since the island crawled

into a continent, I've been
shell and memory, calendar and hearth.

ENDNOTES

"The dead do not bury themselves" is a phrase often used in archaeology and forensic anthropology, without singular attribution.

In "Central Nervous System," the epigraph is a phrase frequently appearing in newspaper reports on protest events, such as Stonewall, Occupy, and Black Lives Matter.

Italicized lines in "Forensics" are an imagined textbook entry, in reference to the collection of nineteenth-century skeletal remains housed at University of Missouri–St. Louis.

Italicized lines in "Draw the Human Form" are an imagined ballet review.

In "Determination of Racial Affinity," the epigraph is a frequently used phrase in forensic anthropology worksheets and presentations, without singular attribution. Lines in stanza five come from a "Can You Identify Ancestry" activity sheet from the Smithsonian Museum of Natural History.

In "Phthisis," "who erased the sea" comes from an English translation of a song title in *La Traviata* ("Who erased the sea, the land of Provence from your heart?").

The epigraph of "In Which I Become (Tiger Lily)" is from the song "What Made the Red Man Red," from Disney's *Peter Pan* (1953).

"In Which I Become (Skywoman)" also takes the form of a contrapuntal, and can be read as a series of vertical poems as well as a singular horizontal line-by-line piece.

The "Letters I Don't Send" include references to Marilyn Monroe and Joe DiMaggio, Japanese folklore and Greek mythology, Yoko Ono, the movie *Death Becomes Her*, and of course, many iterations of an evil queen.

In "All I Need to Know about Love I Learned from My Fellow Primates," italicized lines are an imagined textbook entry based on ethological studies of titi monkeys. Callitrichids (including marmosets) and *Callicebus* (titi monkeys) tend to form monogamous pairs, whereas ring-tailed lemurs form polyandrous harems, and orangutans have a semi-solitary noyau social structure—although this last could also potentially be attributed to habitat loss.

"Ode to Lookouts and Lighthouse Keepers" is in response to volunteer work at the Sand Mountain Fire Lookout in the Oregon Cascades, and to a visit to the Obrestad Lighthouse on the Jæren coast of Norway (a site of Norwegian resistance and later German occupation during World War II), with appreciation to the Sand Mountain Society's continuing efforts to restore historic fire lookouts and to the municipal government of Hå for their caretaking of the Obrestad Lighthouse.

In "Love Song to Banish Another Love Song," the first line refers to a Spanish proverb, *un clavo saca otro clavo*. It has also been attributed to Erasmus (*clavum clavo pellere*).

"When I Say I Love You, This Is What I Mean" includes a reference to the Forbes Pigment Collection at the Harvard Art Museums.

CREDITS

With gratitude to the venues in which the following poems first appeared:

The Adroit Journal, "Elegy against Elegy," "In Which I Become
(Earth Mother)," "Love Song to the Alpacas of Solomon
Lane," "When I Say I Love You, This Is What I Mean"

Alphabeast: A Book of Poems, "With Thirteen Moons on Your Back"

Apogee, "Determination of Racial Affinity"

Blue Earth Review, "Draw the Human Form"

The Boiler, "Letters I Don't Send #1,"
"Letters I Don't Send #2," "Letters I Don't Send #7"

Boston Review, "How the Skin Bruises If You
Lie There Long Enough," "Token"

Cleaver, "Letters I Don't Send #5" (originally #4), "Light Pollution"

Dialogist, "Dress Like Pocahontas, Then Let's Make Love"

Drunken Boat, "Illiterate"

*Embodied: An Intersectional Feminist Comics
Poetry Anthology,* "Red Woman"

The Ex-Puritan, "Repatriation"

Four Winds, "In Which I Become (Tiger Lily)"

HAD, "Remnants"

Horse Less Review, "Ribbons"

Indiana Review, "Psychomanteum"

The Iowa Review, "Forensics," "Pathology"

Iron Horse Literary Review, "Letters I Don't Send #3"

Narrative, "How to Be a Real Indian," "Love Song to the Man Announcing Pow Wows and Rodeos," "Whatever Is the Matter"

The Paris Review's The Daily, "Quiet as Thunderbolts"

The Rumpus, "Convergent Evolution"

Santa Ana River Review, "Piano Factory" (as "West 46th between 9 and 10")

SOFTBLOW, "Ask Me How It Happened," "Letters I Don't Send #4" (originally #5)

Word Riot, "Palm Reader, Fifth Avenue"

ACKNOWLEDGMENTS

With much appreciation, this collection has been supported by Vermont Studio Center, Hedgebrook, the Elizabeth Murray Artist Residency, Disquiet International, 92NY, Aspen Summer Words, Indigenous Nations Poets, and the Hopwood Awards Program.

To Michael Mercurio and Minadora Macheret, thank you for your care in reading this book at each step along the way and for your unfailing encouragement. Likewise, thank you to Anthony Madrid for every letter and birthday poem you've ever written me, and to Shannon Elizabeth Hardwick and Michael Mlekoday for encouraging me from the very start. To David Goldstein, Jeanne Obbard, David Lu, Brendan Ford, Mary-Alice Daniel, Chigozie Obioma, Ahimsa Timoteo Bodhrán, Brandon Amico, Alyse Bensel, Charlotte Dunn, and Meredith Luby, thank you for the gift of your friendship.

I am grateful for the guidance and support of the University of Michigan's Helen Zell Writers' Program and Laura Kasischke, Khaled Mattawa, Keith Taylor, and A. Van Jordan; the University of Wisconsin-Milwaukee's Creative Writing Program and Brenda Cárdenas, Kimberly M. Blaeser, Rebecca Dunham, Lane Hall, Michael Wilson, and Bernard C. Perley; my anthropology professors at Washington University in St. Louis, including Robert Sussman, D. Tab Rasmussen, and archaeological field school director, John E. Kelly; and always, Kerri Webster.

To Craig Santos Perez, Heid E. Erdrich, and Diane Seuss, thank you for the shining example of your work and for your kind words toward this book.

Thank you to all the Tin House team, including Beth Steidle, Becky Kraemer, Nanci McCloskey, Jae Nichelle, Jacqui Reiko Teruya, Masie Cochran, David Caligiuri, and editor extraordinaire, Alyssa Ogi, for seeing the possibilities in these poems and for helping to shepherd them into the world.

To my grandmother, and to our giver of names, Yakeyale (Maria Hinton), to Toni House and all my aunties, to Hugh and Michelle Danforth and Leah Stroobants and Norbert Hill, Jr., to Brian Doxtator for each story he shared, and to the Oneida Nation of Wisconsin, thank you, *yawʌkó*, for teaching me to move in good ways. Thank you to the land and all our relations.

To my mom and dad, thank you for the gift of my life; and for the love of the natural world, the cultural inheritances, the courage, that shaped me and in turn shaped this book. Dad, *now* you can start asking about the next book. Thank you and much love to Diana, Katie, Donnie, and all our family.

To *min kjære*, Andreas, thank you for being my best reader and my best beloved. To my daughter, Sahalie, I'm so grateful for all the new love songs you inspire.

Thank you to the late Kenneth E. Harrison, Jr., for being such a wonderful mentor, poet, and friend.

Kenzie Allen is a Haudenosaunee poet and multimodal artist. A finalist for the National Poetry Series, her work has appeared in *Poetry* magazine, *Boston Review*, *Narrative*, *The Paris Review*'s The Daily, *Best New Poets*, Poets.org, and other venues. Born in West Texas, she now shares time between Toronto, Ontario; Stavanger, Norway; and the Oneida reservation in Green Bay, Wisconsin.